YOU WO GET RICH, BEING AN IDIOT!

BADBOY Publishing
www.BadboyPublishing.com

JOSEPH M. WARREN

YOU WON'T
GET RICH,
BEING AN
IDIOT!

◆

7 "Idiot-Proof" Strategies
Small Business Owners Can Use
To <u>Stop Wasting Money</u>
On Stupid Stuff

◆

JOSEPH WARREN
and JASON STOLL

Produced by:
BADBOY Publishing - www.BadboyPublishing.com

Edited by:
Joseph Warren & Jason Stoll

Book Cover Designed by:
Andrew "AJ" Favicchio - www.SauceOnTap.com

Cover Photograph by:
Leandro Gongora - www.GongoraPhotography.com

ISBN:0692351647
ISBN-13: 9780692351642

"Business success is more than luck; it's about not being an **idiot**."

~ Joseph Warren

JOSEPH M. WARREN

To hire Joseph Warren to speak at
your next event, please visit:
www.JosephWarren.net

DISCLAIMER

This book is designed to provide information on business and entrepreneurship only. This information is provided and sold with the knowledge that the publisher and author do not offer any legal, financial, or medical advice. In the case of a need for any such expertise consult with the appropriate professional. This book does not contain all information available on the subject. This book has not been created to be specific to any individual people or organizations' situation or needs. Reasonable efforts have been made to make this book as accurate as possible. However, there may be typographical and or content errors. Therefore, this book should serve only as a general guide and not as the ultimate source of subject information. This book contains information that might be dated or erroneous and is intended only to educate and entertain. The author and publisher shall have no liability or responsibility to any person or entity regarding any loss or damage incurred, or alleged to have incurred, directly or indirectly, by the information contained in this book or as a result of anyone acting or failing to act upon the information in this book. You hereby agree never to sue and to hold the author and publisher harmless from any and all claims arising out of the information contained in this book. You hereby agree to be bound by this disclaimer, covenant not to sue and release. You may return this book within the guarantee time period for a full refund. In the interest of full disclosure, this book contains affiliate links that might pay the author or publisher a commission upon any purchase from the company. While the author and publisher take no responsibility for any virus or technical issues that could be caused by such kinks, the business practices of these companies and or the performance of any product or service, the author or publisher has used the product or service and makes a recommendation in good faith based on that experience.

All characters appearing in this work are real people.

DEDICATION

Jason Stoll, thank you for walking this crazy startup journey with me.

So many unexpected twists and turns, yet somehow we've managed to hang onto this entrepreneurial rollercoaster and not give up.

Ten thousand hours of blood, sweat, and tears later; the simple idea of creating "a better place to work" has launched CoCreativ on its path towards becoming a national chain of shared workspaces where entrepreneurs can start, launch, or grow their businesses.

Here's to the future my friend, to the unknown adventure that lies ahead of us.

May we beat the odds and win the race.

JOSEPH M. WARREN

CONTENTS

JOSEPH M. WARREN

ACKNOWLEDGMENTS

Jared Ganem:
Humble and ready to hustle.
www.CreativeInnovationsVideo.com
(page 35)

Marco Midence:
Friendly, Reliable and Consistent.
www.TacticalTechnologiesUSA.com
(page 49)

Eddie de la Rosa:
Simply professional.
www.BacasoConsulting.com
(page 58)

Molly Smith:
Always a pleasure to speak with.
www.College2Career.us
(page 69)

Elizabeth Fanslow:
Gracious, kind and fun.
www.ElizabethFanslow.com
(page 74)

Sheri Taber:
Mentor, client and friend.
www.ThePPGinc.com
(page 81)

Jennifer Samuel-Chance:
Aka "Miss Jen Jen" and dearest friend.
www.linkedin.com/in/jennifersamuelchance
(page 93)

Alan & Peter Akman:
Climbing the "tech mountain".
www.Raxar.com
(page 97)

Dan Ross:
Always there for a good laugh.
www.Med-Vision.com
(page 107)

Andrew Favicchio:
Hustle and integrity.
www.SauceOnTap.com
(page 117)

INTRODUCTION

Passion won't pay your bills.

Everyone says that you should follow your passion. That's great advice, but is it enough?

Hell no. If you believe that, then you're an idiot.

I think we can all agree that having passion for what you do is incredibly important because it helps you get through the tough times.

It helps you communicate your vision to others in a way that gets them on board and excited about helping you get there.

We all agree that passion is important. However, here's the problem:

It takes more than passion and a great idea to build a **successful business.**

Starting, launching and growing a business takes guts, smarts, and determination. Lots of it.

Another thing you'll need is to be <u>obsessed with cutting costs.</u>

One of the fastest ways to increase profit in your new business is to cut your overhead costs.

When you lower expenses, you're left with more cash in your pockets.

The problem is that most newbie business owners are constantly **increasing** their expenses because <u>they spend their hard-earned cash on really dumb things</u>.

Does that $5 latte really taste better than saving on office space?

Does that fancy-looking company logo and website you paid some marketing company four grand to create really land you more clients?

Does that PO Box at the UPS Store really make you look more professional?

Any seasoned entrepreneur can tell you about the pain, struggles, and sacrifice of building a business.

As a new business owner, you'll have to say goodbye to the security that comes from receiving a steady paycheck you can count on every month.

As a new business owner, you'll have to say hello to the long hours that you'll put in when you'd rather be out partying with your friends.

There's really nothing sexy about running a business except for the fact that you're running a business.

It's work. It's pain.

Success comes from doing what needs to get done regardless of whether you feel like doing it.

Your business doesn't care that you're feeling "under the weather", or unmotivated due to the fact that you're over-worked or underpaid.

It doesn't care that you are frustrated or exhausted, happy, or sad.

All that matters is that you show up day after day and do the work.

Many days you'll want to give up, throw in the towel, and quit.

But you can't, you won't. You're better than that.

So how will you stay motivated for the next 3-5 years that it takes to build your business?

To stay motivated and on track, you'll need to surround yourself with other productive people who are going through (or have been through) the same or similar challenges as you.

Imagine. Imagine leaving your home office and all its distractions behind, and driving to a place bustling with new and seasoned business owners just like you.

A shared workspace where everyone shares their time, energy and resources for the benefit of all ------ that's **coworking**.

With that in mind, here's what's unique and different about coworking.

Some of the people who work at a coworking space may be a few "exits" past you on the startup highway and are more than willing to help you avoid the same costly mistakes they've already made.

Here's what's good about that.

You'll save time, energy and resources, which will help accelerate your success.

That means you'll get to keep the few greenbacks that you still have in your wallet.

It means that you'll spend less time on meaningless tasks and more time on cash-producing tasks.

And it means that you'll get to hit your goals faster and with more accuracy.

You'll learn. You'll grow. You'll win.

That's just one benefit of coworking.

To find out the second, the third, and the fourth benefit of coworking, start reading Chapter One now.

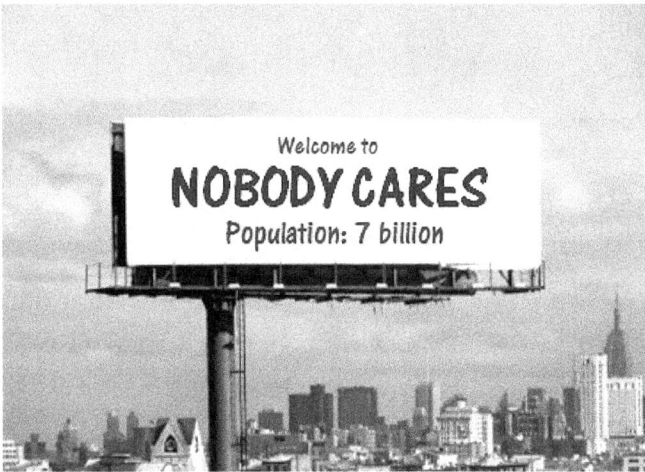

YOU WON'T GET RICH
BEING AN **EGOMANIAC**

There are 7 billion people on the planet ----- *and then there's you.*

That's 7,000,000,000 people who have their own needs, pain, struggles, divorces, unemployment, health problems, depression, anxiety, relationship problems, addictions, money problems, etc.....

So why on earth would anyone care about you?

C'mon you know it's a fair question.

Not only is it fair but it's the BIG question that you should be answering before you ever pull the trigger and start a new business.

You're probably thinking to yourself; well I know I can get <u>some people</u> to care. No you can't. And if you think you can, then you're an idiot.

They don't care and they never will, so stop thinking like an idiot and open up your mind.

Starting a new business is only for people with thick skin so if my last comment offended you then you should put down this book, go throw your entrepreneurial delusions out the window, and get back to working for someone else.

But that's not you; you're tougher than that right?

You're a fighter, a scrapper, and you won't go down without a fight. You've sacrificed short-term cravings with the hopes of getting that elusive pot of gold at the end of the small business rainbow.

I bet you've been through a lot lately. After all, you're just one of the 7 billion people who have their own problems... and that's exactly why you CAN and will succeed.

But first you'll have to suck it up, put on your big girl panties, and swallow a serious dose of intense reality!

Ready? Here it comes…

People don't care about you. They care about themselves and their problems.

Still you'll be tempted to spend 99% of your time, energy and resources on telling the world how great you and your products are instead of <u>showing them how you can remove their pain</u>.

You'll be more concerned about getting your fancy company name and logo just right, than you will be about understanding your customers and identifying what they're desperately searching for.

Why? Like most business owners, you'll love your company name and logo more than your customer. That's right, I said it.

You'll say it's for branding purposes but that's a lie. It's really about your ego and how emotionally attached you'll become to your own junk.

You'll get drunk on your own "Kool Aid".

Plus since everyone else is doing it, it must be good right? Again, you're an idiot.

But let's not forget about your cute pictures, corny slogans and boring-ass product features that you'll slap all over your website, business cards, and every other available surface.

That should get their attention, right?

Wrong.

Nobody cares. People only care about THEMSELVES AND THEIR PROBLEMS.

Speak about your customer's fears and you'll open their ears.

Speak about their problems and they'll listen to just about everything you have to say. Speak about yourself and they'll listen to nothing.

People don't care about you. They care about themselves and their problems.

--- **IDIOT LESSON** ---

Don't Be An Egomaniac:

The world doesn't care about you or your fancy-schmancy product. People care about themselves. The sooner you accept that fact, the more successful you will be.

Unless you want us to throw you a pity party. Fine. We'll send you the bill.

YOU WON'T GET RICH
SMOKING POT

Working from home is like smoking pot, everyone's doing it but no one wants to admit it.

And like many naïve business owners, you'll try the home office at least once because the promise of freedom outweighs the truth.

And then like many newbie business owners, you'll soon find out that you're an idiot.

But who can blame you?

Initially you'll be lured in by the promise of freedom, the carefreeness of working and sleeping whenever you want, the nostalgia of sliding through the workday in your pajamas, or the perceived danger of stealing random deliciousness from the fridge.

No boss
looking over
your shoulder.
No time clock
to punch.
No coworkers
to avoid.
No traffic to give
your finger to.

Nope, nothing but you and your bedroom mirror. And that's the problem…

You need accountability. Admit it, you're not disciplined enough to create a detailed work schedule and stick to it.

--- CASE STUDY ---

www.CreativeInnovationsVideo.com

Jared Ganem is founder and CEO of Fight Sports HD in Tampa, Florida. He started his video production company out of his home in January 2014.

Initially, he liked the thought of setting his own schedule, making breakfast in the morning, and then starting work whenever he wanted.

But he found it difficult to separate his business and home life. It was nearly impossible to "shut it off".

"Even though I was working from home and making good money, I didn't feel successful. I procrastinated more at home. I felt like a loser. Does my wife think I'm a bum?"

So he contacted our company and signed up for a private office with 24/7 access to grow his video production business. We helped him by providing him with his own 10'x10' window office, open shared workspace, private meeting rooms, soft lighting, plus the freedom and free flow of energy, as well as, targeted introductions to grow his business.

Now he drives to his professional office space to be productive and meet with clients.

"It's a way to have a business with very low overhead, it keeps my operation lean. Plus it makes my business more real."

He no longer feels obligated to answer client emails and phone calls "after hours" and then work on them. It can wait until the next day when he gets to the office.

"CoCreativ provided a clear balance where I can turn off 'work mode' on the way home. It creates a boundary and has greatly improved my mental state so that I feel better with clients, have more confidence, and I am more productive."

Even his wife is happy with his decision to move his office out of their home.

"My wife encourages this. She says my mental state is better. One time she said, 'Don't ever give this up! Don't look at it as an expense; look at it as an investment.'"

Jared is just one of millions of new business owners who learned the hard way that working from home isn't as pretty as it looks.

"Now my house is actually my house again. I needed that separation."

Today, Jared is landing huge video production gigs around the world. He went from a one-man home business in Tampa, Florida to an international business in less than 9 months. He and his team just got flown to London to do a video shoot for his largest client ever.

Not bad for a former wrestler with no previous business experience.

--- IDIOT LESSON ---

Don't Be A Stoner:

You need a separation between work and home, between your office and your bedroom.

It's time to turn off "work mode" and spend more time doing what you love with the peeps who matter most to you. It will make your life really groovy, man.

JOSEPH M. WARREN

YOU WON'T GET RICH BEING A **CAFFEINE** **JUNKIE**

Meeting clients at coffee shops screams,
"I can't afford an office!"

Translation: Your customers are thinking that you can't afford an office because no one is hiring you. And if no one else is hiring you, why should they?

Of course we both know this isn't true, but <u>what you and I think doesn't really matter</u>, does it?

All that matters is what your customers think when they think about you.

That's your brand.

When your customers speak about you to their friends, do you really want them saying, "His office is the Starbucks on 4th street"!?!?

You must be joking.

Maybe you still think there's nothing wrong with meeting your clients at the coffee shop.

Yup, you're still an idiot.

Have you ever seen
someone write a
$10,000 check
in a coffee shop?
Me neither.
That's because it
never happens.

Business doesn't happen in coffee shops. **Loss of business happens in coffee shops.** First you lose credibility with your client, and then you lose their business.

LESSON: Coffee shops are good for personal meetings but BAD for business.

--- CASE STUDY ---

www.TacticalTechnologiesUSA.com

Marco Midence owns Tactical Technologies in Tampa, Florida. Tactical Technologies is a Discount Gun Shop specializing in the transfer and sale of firearms.

His business caters to the firearm purchaser who does not want to pay full retail prices.

In order to stand out and differentiate his company in an overcrowded marketplace, Marco contacted our company for private meeting rooms in Tampa to meet his customers and vendors.

He also signed up for a virtual business address and mail services so that his clients' orders can be shipped directly to our facility before his scheduled meetings.

This unique business model allows his company to sell any firearm for only 10% over invoice.

[Most local gun stores charge 20% - 30% over invoice due to their large overhead costs which include leases on large retail showrooms and employee salaries.]

Since Marco leverages "just in time inventory", and uses our office space and meeting rooms rather than costly retail space, he is in a unique position to offer customers <u>highly discounted pricing</u>.

Imagine how much money he is saving by streamlining his business like this and not carrying the crushing overhead of leasing an office or retail location.

This creates more revenue running through his company and more cash filling his pockets.

Due to his competitive pricing, Marco has attracted so many new customers that he recently inquired about renting our 24-person training room so that he can provide firearm certification classes as an additional service to his customers.

At $150 a head, he is sure to pack the room (and his wallet).

Do you really think Marco would be this successful if he conducted his client meetings at a coffee shop??

Now you're getting it.

--- IDIOT LESSON ---

Don't Be A Caffeine Junkie:

You're never going to get rich trying to save a few bucks using the coffee shop as your office. That's for lame-ass losers.

Paying for a real workplace is an investment in your business and your success. Don't believe it? Fine. Feel free to remain an idiot.

YOU WON'T GET RICH BEING A **DUMB-ASS**

Congratulations, BAD people now know where you live!

Putting your home address on your business license, or business formation (LLC) documents is a stupid idea.

This is all public record.

This means that anyone good, bad, criminal, or dangerous can now find out where you live.

Yes I know, someone told you it was a good idea. Oh and let's not forget that everyone else is doing it too, right? Sorry, no free pass this time.

You're an even bigger idiot than before.

I hope you have a gun in the house for when that crazy customer (you know the type) comes banging on your door when you're not there but your kids are!?!?

Shame on you for doing something as dangerous as inviting every creep in town to make an unannounced social visit to your home.

You're probably thinking to yourself...

"Joseph, I would never be foolish enough to list my home address online. That's why I got me one of those fancy-schmancy P.O. Boxes at the Post Office (or UPS Store)."

Well congratulations, you're officially a **dumb-ass**.

Nowadays when people see a P.O. Box listed on your website or business card, <u>they immediately think that you're trying to HIDE something</u>.

It's true and I can prove it.

Imagine doing a Google search for *"virtual office space in Tampa"*, seeing our website CoCreativ.com listed on top, and then clicking to find our location.

Which of these two addresses would make you NOT want to call us for more information? Which address would make you more skeptical?

CoCreativ
P.O. Box 208
Tampa, FL 33629

vs.

CoCreativ
3902 Henderson Blvd. Suite 208
Tampa, FL 33629

The answer is obvious.

P.O. Boxes are impersonal, unprofessional, and immediately send up "red flags" in your customer's mind.

Seriously, what are you trying to hide?

It's all about TRUST.

The last thing you ever want to do is create a 'red flag' about your company in your customer's mind.

If customers don't trust you,
they won't give you their hard-earned CASH.

--- CASE STUDY ---

www.BacascoConsulting.com

Eddie de la Rosa is a group benefits consultant in Tampa, Florida. Eddie's insurance business was doing well but Eddie wanted to expand his North Tampa business into the South Tampa market.

He contacted our company about our getting a virtual office and mail services to expand his business.

In less than 30 minutes, we set him up with a new business address in South Tampa including a unique suite number dedicated to his business.

A few months later, his business was doing extremely well and he wanted to add affordable legal services to his product offerings.

To do this effectively, he needed to make sure not to confuse his existing insurance customers by adding in legal services.

He felt the best way to do this would be to keep them as separate businesses.

He started a second company that specialized in providing legal services.

Eddie contacted our company again for a virtual address and mail services for his second business.

30 minutes later, he was up and running.

Now both of his companies are successfully positioned in the South Tampa marketplace.

Profits are up,
customers
are happy,
and so is Eddie.

--- IDIOT LESSON ---

Don't Be A Dumb-Ass:

Never ever use your home address or P.O. Box as your business address. Invest in a real business address so that you can look bigger and better than where you are. Let the creeps stalk someone else on Facebook.

JOSEPH M. WARREN

YOU WON'T GET RICH BEING A **HERMIT**

Man was not meant to work alone. And don't even get me started on women; they're already pre-wired for collaboration and *"togetherness"*.

Yep, that's a word.

Working alone is okay for the first few weeks when you're just starting out but eventually it will bite you in your asset ----- your biggest asset ------ **productivity**.

Your productivity will drop like a rock and your clarity will become a thick cloud of confusion.

When this happens, you'll need other brains around you challenging your biased opinions and your un-researched hunches.

If you think you don't, guess what?

You're an idiot.

Name for me one well-recognized company where the founder did everything on their own all the way from the bottom to the top. C'mon name just one?

It doesn't exist.

Everything that's great in the world was built by teams. Maybe one person sparked the idea but it takes a team of people to execute plans into reality.

"Dreams don't come true, plans come true."

~ Larry Winget

--- CASE STUDY ---

www.College2Career.us

Molly Smith is the owner of College2Career in Tampa, FL. South Tampa moms hire Molly to help their high school or college students plan out customized pre-college and post-college career paths.

Molly was SO GOOD at what she did that she would often get invited to speak at parent groups about college and career planning for their students. Hmmm, a room-full of motivated parents ready to buy? Talk about easy pickins!

However, every time Molly got invited, **she would decline**.

She knew that it was a great opportunity to win more clients but she couldn't get herself to do it.

Why not?

Molly was deathly afraid of speaking in front of groups. Glossophobia strikes again :(

This had been going on for years and she needed to take back control of her life. Her fear was adversely affecting her company revenue and profits. Not to mention her confidence.

Molly contacted our company about getting a private office and then joined our in-house Referral Group where small business owners network and share "warm" referrals and leads.

After joining our group, I introduced Molly to **Jennifer Samuel-Chance**, a professional speaker, master storyteller, and my personal speaker coach who helps clients eliminate their public speaking fear and perfect their presentation skills.

"In only a few short sessions, she helped Molly go from <u>severe panic attacks</u> to calm and confident."

Today, Molly is fearless and accepts every speaking invitation, which has led to excellent business opportunities and higher revenue for her company.

What if Molly continued to work from home by herself and never came to us for help?

Well, she wouldn't have been introduced to Jennifer ---- the very person who had the unique solution to her very painful problem.

Goodbye isolation.

--- CASE STUDY ---

www.ElizabethFanslow.com

Elizabeth Fanslow is the owner of a social marketing strategy company in Tampa, FL and the former President of a major online marketing company.

For years she was isolated and confined working from home.

As an *introvert* she needed a focused environment but occasionally liked to hear the noise and buzz of busy people working around her to stimulate her creativity.

"I love the buzz of a coffee shop but there are too many distractions. I needed a place where I could close the door when I needed to work."

Elizabeth contacted our company and grabbed her own private office. She loved the idea of having an office within a shared work environment.

She had visited our facility a couple of times before for business events before making the decision to join.

Our open floor plan gave her the *coffee shop buzz* she was craving yet she could close her door anytime she needed to get heads-down productive.

When she needs to meet a client, she simply pops into one of our meeting rooms.

"This is my Starbucks. I tell people all the time, meet me at CoCreativ."

Now Elizabeth has more clients than ever and her company is growing quickly. She just hired her first assistant to help manage all her new clients.

Elizabeth can often be seen outside her office asking other members for feedback about her ideas.

More than just great collaboration, she found the assistance, mentorship, and community she needed to grow her small business.

Hello inspiration.

--- IDIOT LESSON ---

Don't Be A Hermit:

Constant isolation hurts your productivity, and lets you get caught up in all your "great" ideas even though they're really crap. Go to a place where you can collaborate with others, get some objective feedback, and be inspired to work hard. If you do all that and your ideas are still crap, then maybe you really are an idiot. Sorry about that.

JOSEPH M. WARREN

YOU WON'T GET RICH BEING A **LONE RANGER**

Admit it, you suck at sales! But I bet you're great at something else, right?

No need to get offended miss Shirley Sensitive. Most business owners are terrible at selling.

In the past, selling was reserved for thick-skinned people who could take massive amounts of rejection without getting deflated.

But not anymore.

Starting out, <u>most business owners have to sell</u> because there's no one else to do it but them.

At least for the first few months, you'll be your only salesperson but as your company revenue rises, you'll want to hire a seasoned sales person to bring in more customers.

--- CASE STUDY ---

www.ThePPGinc.com

Sheri' Taber is the CEO of The Peak Performance Group, Inc, a global management consulting, executive development and thought leadership firm in Tampa, Florida.

Sheri had worked alone from home for 30 years but due to her recent business success, was ready to move into a private office space and hire four new sales professionals for 2015 so she could focus her energies on client engagement rather than sales.

She knew she couldn't do it alone. It was time to find a real office where she could provide professional workspace for herself and her sales team.

She heard about our company three times within a ten day period and was prompted by colleagues to come check it out.

She contacted our company for **a private office and workspace for her team.**

As a female, one of her biggest concerns was **safety** going in and out of her office. She also wanted a clean and comfortable environment that was responsive to her business needs.

She loved the idea that she could have a private office for herself, as well as use of our shared workspace for her on-the-road sales professionals before and after their sales appointments.

Her team could drop-in, write proposals, sift through emails, grab coffee, print documents, or schedule meetings with clients if needed.

Sheri has benefited from exposure to others by creating new relationships, referrals, and more.

"Since joining CoCreativ, I've been told that my energy is different, it's at a whole new level."

She's excited about growing her sales team and now she has the space to do it.

"CoCreativ makes it easy -- --- easy to sign up, easy to work with, easy to get in and out of my office, and with no surprise fees! CoCreativ has been beyond my expectations."

She has already positioned herself
to hit her goals for the upcoming year
(we even hired her to help us grow CoCreativ).

Quantitatively, her four new sales people represent <u>an additional $1M in revenue for her company this year</u>.

--- IDIOT LESSON ---

Don't Be A Lone Ranger:

Know what your strengths are, and partner with others to do what you hate doing. This will amplify your results exponentially. Heck, even the real Lone Ranger had his sidekick Tonto, so what makes you think you're gonna become a legend trying to do everything yourself, Skippy?

JOSEPH M. WARREN

YOU WON'T GET RICH
BEING A **BLOWHARD**

Without referrals, your fancy-schmancy new business will die.

Sure you can market your new business until you're blue in the face, but without people telling people about your product or service, you'll struggle to attract and retain new customers.

Maybe you think that your self-centered posts on Facebook, Twitter, and LinkedIn are enough to bring in customers ----- like you're some kind of giant social magnet.

Not only are you wrong, but now you're a "narcissistic idiot".

You've got a "magnet" alright but you're using the wrong end (the end that repels people).

It's not enough to talk about yourself. You need to get influencers talking about you.

That's called brand positioning.

The best way to get influencers talking about your product or service is to build lasting relationships with them. This creates and almost endless pipeline of referrals back and forth between you and them.

--- CASE STUDY ---

www.MsJenJen.com

Jennifer Samuel-Chance (aka Miss Jen-Jen) is a professional speaker, master storyteller, and speaker coach who resides in Tampa, FL.

She travels nationally and has been on and off of airplanes for about 15 years.

Her daunting travel schedule has been taking its toll on her energy and overall passion for what she loves doing.

She needed a change and wanted to attract more local coaching clients so that she didn't have to travel as often.

She contacted our company about our in-house **Referral Club** to help grow her coaching practice and attract more local clients.

After attending regular meetings and frequenting our shared workspace, she built relationships with 50+ small business owners, many of whom have become her clients.

New customers have been referred to her numerous times locally and she's well on her way to hitting her goal of totally replacing her current income while staying close to home.

This has freed up more time in her schedule and allowed her to shift her lifestyle to the <u>things that really matter to her</u>, such as spending more time with friends and family.

That's called success.

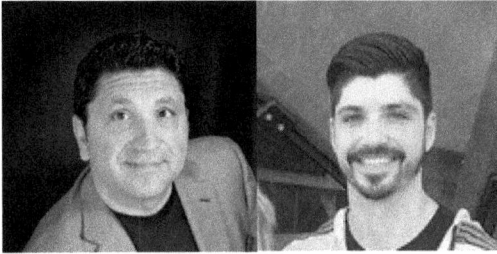

--- CASE STUDY ---

www.Raxar.com

Alan and Peter Akman founded and own RAXAR, a new technology startup in Tampa, Florida, which provides a smart phone app used for the real time inventory, tracking, and inspection of organizational assets.

Alan had already "exited" his first company, which he sold to Autodesk and was revving up to do something similar with RAXAR.

Alan and Peter contacted our company about our **Referral Club** because they needed introductions to key decision makers in their industry.

Alan also requested an introduction to my speaker coach Ms. Jen-Jen so that he could **improve his pitch presentations to prospective investors.**

I introduced them to the sought after connections they were seeking.

Soon doors that were previously closed to them have been consistently flying open.

Now this father and son team is landing the right partners, the right customers, and the right investors who can help take their company closer to "IPO Land".

With investors lining up, soon they'll be spending 30 percent of their time in Tampa and 70 percent of their time in the land of the investor gods ----- San Francisco.

One GREAT introduction can change everything.

I said that.

--- IDIOT LESSON ---

Don't Be A Blowhard:

No one, not even your mother, wants to hear you blab on and on about how great your product is, so stick a cork in it already. Make your product and service so great that your customers can't stop saying good things about it to others. That's when your business will take off. And when your mom hears Ethel and Margaret talking about it at her crochet club, she'll be so proud that she'll cook you a nice big pot of homemade chicken noodle soup. Yum.

JOSEPH M. WARREN

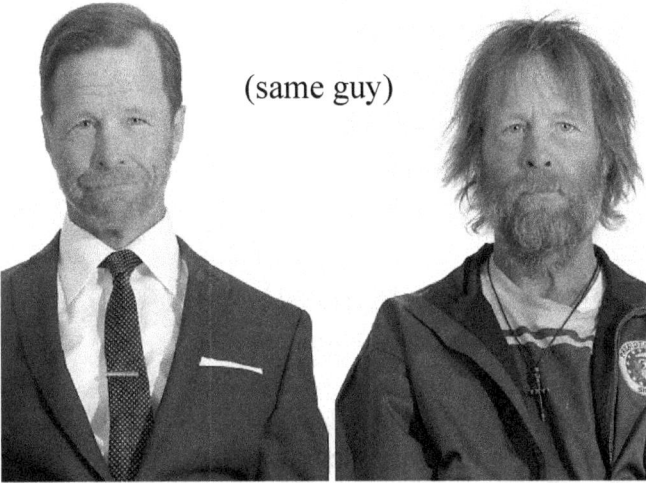

(same guy)

YOU WON'T GET RICH LOOKING LIKE A **BUM**

People will always judge a book by its cover.

People make all types of assumptions based on what they "see" but they rarely take the time to get all the facts.

<u>Customer Perception</u>: If you don't look successful, you're not successful.

And nobody wants to hand over their hard-earned cash to someone who's not successful.

Would you?

In an earlier chapter, we agreed that working from home is like smoking pot ----- everyone's doing it but no one wants to admit it.

People's perception of you working from home is that you're a bum. You're a broke loser. And few people will hire a bum.

Where you work DOES matter. Actually, it matters very much.

It matters almost as much as what you do and even who you are. Your workspace is one of the first impressions people will have of your business.

Impress them and you may earn their business. Disappoint them and you can kiss their CASH goodbye.

Adios. Sayonara. *Au Revoir.*

As an idealist, I used to think that people would see past my shabby-pathetic workspace and unprofessional "Panera-office", and hire me based solely on my great product, personality, or skillset.

I was an idiot. Yup, I can admit it.

--- CASE STUDY ---

www.Med-Vision.com

Dan Ross is CEO of Med-Vision in Tampa, Florida. Med-Vision helps self-funded employers increase earnings while simultaneously improving the health and productivity of employees.

Dan found it challenging to avoid distractions working from his home office, whether it was the kids, pets, or deliveries.

He also didn't like the perception of using his home address as his business address, which hampered success at closing larger prospective clients.

Dan was introduced to CoCreativ by one of his friends who recently became a member himself. Dan was immediately captivated by the openness of the space and friendliness of the people there, and took an office on the spot.

Dan was tired of working at home and needed a place to work with **no office politics**, or negative atmosphere.

He was tired of the snotty, **elitist**, superficial, loud, and **overly-crowded** workspaces where it's nearly impossible to get a meeting room.

He wanted an open easy atmosphere instead of a cubicle farm.

Simply put, **he wanted office freedom.**

He contacted our company about a private office for himself and his sales team so they could call on doctors all day long.

"The thing about sales is that it's the highest of highs and the lowest of lows."

"Here there is someone to celebrate with and someone to cry with."

But Dan wanted more than a great place to hang his sales cap ----- **he wanted an office perception that matched where his company was headed,** not where it was.

"All men need a place to go outside their house. Nobody ever says their office is cool, but here I can say that. Our office is part of our brand identity."

The perception of having a real office versus a home office can be the difference between your company standing a fighting chance in a dog-eat-dog startup world, or becoming part of the staggering statistics of failed startup businesses dumped into the loser ditch.

"CoCreativ is the next step for your home business."

--- IDIOT LESSON ---

Don't Look Like A Bum:

Your workspace says just as much about you as your appearance – if it looks shoddy, you're a bum in the eyes of others. Look the part and get a real office. Unless you want complete strangers to randomly give you dollar bills and point you in the direction of the nearest homeless shelter. Ouch. That's cold.

--- CASE STUDY ---

www.SauceOnTap.com

Andrew "AJ" Favicchio is founder of Sauce Digital LLC in Tampa, FL.

After graduating the University of Tampa, AJ contacted our company to inquire if we needed video work done to help promote our brand.

After seeing the quality of his video work and his "eye" for design, I brought AJ on as an <u>unpaid intern</u>. Within months, I was introducing AJ to our other small business members who instantly hired him to create marketing videos for their companies.

Because AJ came so highly recommended by me and did such great work, it got to the point that he would come into CoCreativ to edit videos and other members would walk over to his desk and hire him on the spot.

Literally all he had to do to land <u>new paying clients</u>, was show up each day!!!

Soon he had so many clients that he decided to turn it into a real business and form his own LLC.

Today AJ is landing large enterprise clients and off to building the business of his dreams!

Not bad for a 23 year college graduate who took the initiative to put himself in the right business environment and show us what he could do.

Taking bold initiative trumps unemployment.

Checkmate.

Summary

Alrighty then, let's recap all the ways in which you're currently an idiot:

- *You won't get rich being an egomaniac.*
- *You won't get rich smoking pot.*
- *You won't get rich being a caffeine junkie.*
- *You won't get rich being a dumb-ass.*
- *You won't get rich being a hermit.*
- *You won't get rich being a lone ranger.*
- *You won't get rich being a blowhard.*
- *You won't get rich looking like a bum.*

I know what you're thinking: "Geez, I really suck – I'm an idiot and I'm not rich." But wait, there's still hope for you.

"So how do I become rich?"

Well, if you want to become rich, marry a sugar daddy.

"Gee, thanks. Well then how do I <u>not</u> be an idiot?" Here's what to do:

- *Accept that the world doesn't care about you; they care about themselves.*
- *Distinguish your professional life from your personal life. Forget about work-life balance; instead focus on work-life integration.*
- *Ditch the coffee shop and use professional meeting rooms.*
- *Get a real business address.*
- *Collaborate with others and get some feedback and useful advice.*
- *Partner with others whose strengths complement yours.*
- *Develop raving fans who can't stop talking about your product to others.*
- *Invest in a professional-looking office; it will raise your appearance considerably.*

There are no guarantees in life, but if you do all of these things, you'll definitely give yourself the best chance for success. And you'll be miles ahead of the idiots still schlepping along trying to be cheap or thinking they're the center of the known universe.

We all know how that turns out.

So what are you waiting for, a hand-written invitation? Get to it! Unless you prefer staying an idiot ;)

JOSEPH M. WARREN

ABOUT THE AUTHOR

JOSEPH M. WARREN
Co-Founder & CEO
CoCreativ.com

AUTHOR I SPEAKER I ENTREPRENEUR

Started $2M business at age 19. Cheated death twice. Broke and homeless by 27. Crushed fear of public speaking. Co-Founded CoCreativ, a future national chain of shared workspaces. Published author. Speaks to thousands of college students about how to get hired or start a business after college.

Raised by a single mother on welfare, Joseph Warren dreaded their weekly trips to the supermarket and hung his head in shame as they paid for the family's groceries with Food Stamps®.

He made a commitment to himself that when he became a man, his life would be different... he would be happy, healthy and wealthy.

At age 19, Joseph opened a professional fundraising company that specialized in raising funds for non-profit organizations such as The National Center for Missing & Exploited Children (NCMEC). Within the first 12 months, he grew his startup into a 50-person firm with $2M+ in revenue. Over the next 24 months, he scaled the business into multiple cities and tripled its revenue.

Joseph Warren (along with renowned speaker and author Dr. Alexander Osterwalder and 470 strategy practitioners) co-authored the groundbreaking and best-selling book, "Business Model Generation - A Handbook for Visionaries, Game Changers, and Challengers".

Business Model Generation has become a practical innovation handbook used today by leading consultants and companies worldwide, including IBM, Ericsson, 3M, Intel, MasterCard, Deloitte, NASA and many others.

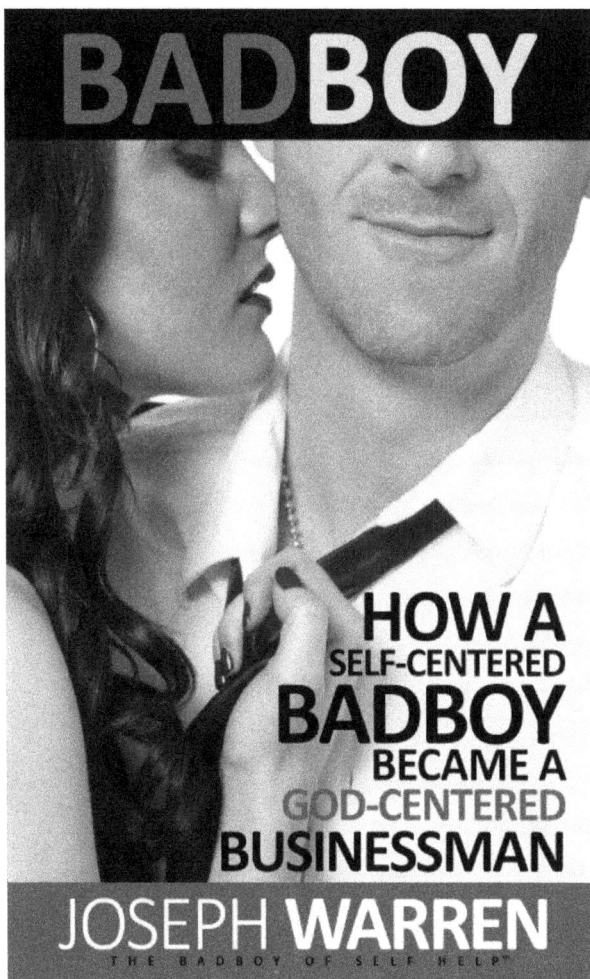
Want more Joseph?

Grab a copy of Joseph's popular book
"BADBOY" available on Amazon &
BarnesAndNoble.com.

JOSEPH M. WARREN

ABOUT THE CO-AUTHOR

JASON STOLL
Co-Founder & COO
CoCreativ.com

OPERATIONS I ENTREPRENEUR

Jason has 15+ years in operations and process improvement. He was instrumental in creating the CoCreativ business plan, pitch, budgeting, and financial projections.

Previously, he served at Coca Cola Refreshments as Business Process Improvement Manager.

He supported large scale integration efforts in terms of process characterization and project management, and also a large scale employee relations capacity improvement initiative.

Before that, Jason worked at <u>Tech Data Corporation</u> in Clearwater, FL. Serving as a Lean Sigma Manager, he developed training programs for over 700 people, including a Lean simulation game enjoyed by all. He was responsible for leading numerous projects with successful results, including a $2 million improvement in working capital and 45% improvement on new item setup lead times.

Prior to that, Jason worked at Ideal-Tomkins PLC in St. Augustine, FL. During his tenure he performed various roles in Quality, Six Sigma, and Lean Manufacturing, and has led several Kaizen Blitzes.

Jason's achievements: (1) Improved productivity by 75% in a work cell, (2) $170,000 cost avoidance in manufacturing, (3) Reduced changeover time by 66% in assembly, (4) $42,000 cost savings in tooling, (5) 75% reduction in shipping errors.

Jason holds an MBA from the University of Florida, and a Physics degree from SUNY Fredonia.

JOSEPH M. WARREN

YOU WON'T GET RICH BEING AN IDIOT ™